# The Moral Basis of Democracy

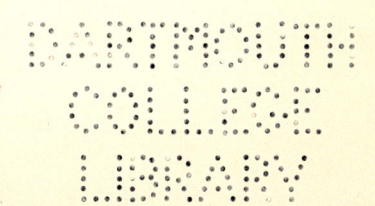

Eleanor Roosevelt

# THE MORAL BASIS OF DEMOCRACY

*hs*

HOWELL, SOSKIN & CO. · NEW YORK

Copyright, 1940, by Eleanor Roosevelt

ALL RIGHTS RESERVED

This book, or any part thereof, may not be reproduced in any form without permission of the publisher

Manufactured in the U. S. A. by American Book–Stratford Press

... I am hoping in this little book to be able to give a clearer definition of the thinking of one citizen in a Democracy. By so doing it may be possible to stimulate the thoughts of many people so that they will force themselves to decide what Democracy means to them—whether they can believe in it as fervently as they can in their personal religion; whether it is worth a sacrifice to them, and what they consider that sacrifice must be.

*E. R.*

*The Moral Basis of Democracy*

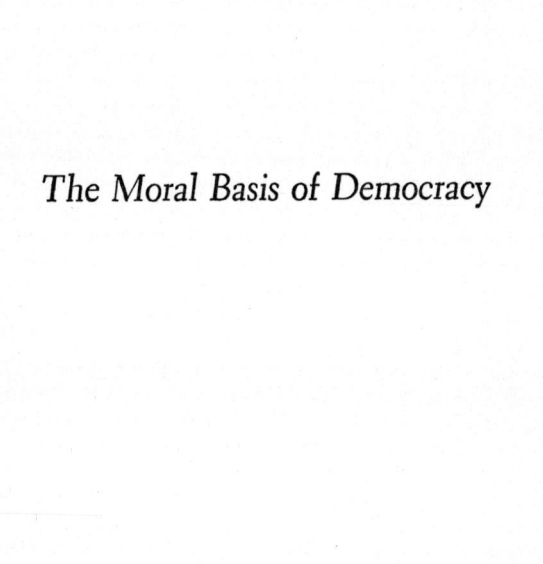

# 1.

AT A TIME when the whole world is in a turmoil and thousands of people are homeless and hungry, it behooves all of us to reconsider our political and religious beliefs in an effort to clarify in our minds the standards by which we live.

What does Democracy mean to any of us? What do we know of its history? Are there any religious beliefs which are essential to the Democratic way of life?

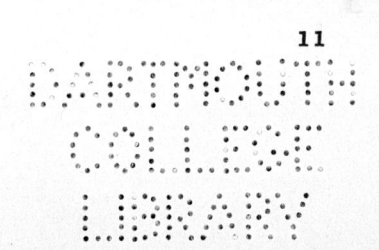

All of these things have been considered and written about, by many historians. I could not possibly write with as wide a background of historical or philosophical knowledge, but I am hoping in this little book to be able to give a clearer definition of the thinking of one citizen in a Democracy. By so doing it may be possible to stimulate the thoughts of many people so that they will force themselves to decide what Democracy means to them—whether they can believe in it as fervently as they can in their personal religion; whether it is worth a sacrifice to them, and what they consider that sacrifice must be.

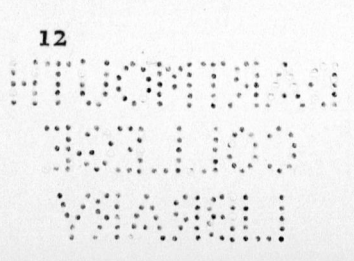

Our Democracy in this country had its roots in religious belief, and we had to acknowledge soon after its birth that differences in religious belief are inherent in the spirit of true Democracy. Just because so many beliefs flourished side by side, we were forced to accept the fact that "a belief" was important, but "what belief" was important only to the individual concerned. Later it was accepted that an individual in this land of ours had the right to any religion, or to no religion. The principle, however, of the responsibility of the individual for the well-being of his neighbors which is akin to: "Love thy neighbor as thyself," in the New Testament, seems always to have been a part of the development of the Democratic ideal which has differentiated it from all other forms of government.

Today, as we look at the various philosophies of government under which people live, the totalitarian state makes the individual of little importance. What he means to the state is paramount. Under the Communist ideal the individual again disappears in the group. Under present conditions both theories of government—the Nazi and the Communist—are practically the same. The will of one man, a dictator, seems to become the will of the state, and because people are not considered as individuals, they merge their will in devotion and submission to the force of the state and of the man who is the symbol of power.

This conception of the state emasculates the

fundamental idea of self-confidence which arises out of individual liberty and for which men have died. Instead, as in the old days when the serf depended on his master, these new serfs depend on their leaders. They live well or ill, in proportion to the degree to which they conform to the will of the master. This was equally true of the medieval barons and their serfs.

The Democratic theory of government and of life in a Democracy opposes one-man rule, and holds to the belief that the individual controls his government through active participation in the processes of political Democratic government, but bows to the will of the majority, freely expressed. The motivating force of the theory of a Democratic way of life is still a belief that as individuals we live co-operatively, and, to the best of our ability, serve the community in which we live, and that our own success, to be real, must contribute to the success of others.

I think this belief can be more firmly grounded through a study of the past, and the principles on which we are now charting our future course can be more clearly defined through a better understanding of the development of Democracy in other countries and eventually in our own.

Therefore, very briefly, we will take a look back into the past.

# 2.

UP TO THE year 1500, there is little or no evidence that anybody gave any thought whatever to the theories of Democracy, but certain basic acts paved the way for the development of practical and theoretical Democracy.

The Magna Charta was the first document drawn up on the theory of Democracy and many of its provisions are now of no more than historical interest. There are, however, many articles which are of continuing importance and current interest. For instance: No taxes shall be imposed except by common counsel. No man shall be imprisoned, exiled or destroyed except by the lawful judgment of his peers or by the law of the land. To no one is right or justice sold or refused. All persons except outlaws or prisoners are free to come and to go, free to buy and to sell, except in time of war.

One of the most important provisions in the Magna Charta is that "The English Church shall be free and shall have her rights entire and her liberties inviolate." Many of the articles in it were directed against the abuses of the power of the King and against many grievances which existed because of feudal tenures.

In 1628 a Petition of Rights was signed, and in 1689 a Bill of Rights was signed.

From 1500 to 1700 in Europe, the development was very slow, but the idea of Democracy seemed to be steadily germinating. By 1750 the idea was firmly implanted in the minds of certain radical thinkers—radical, of course, for their period.

The first real growing pains of Democracy might be considered to spring from English oppression, primarily oppression of religious minority groups, which forced certain free thinkers in England to take refuge first in Holland, which was a tolerant country, but where life was none too easy, and later in the new world across the sea. This land was talked about as the place where one could carve out a future according to new, liberal ideas even though one still owed allegiance to the King of England. These daring and adventurous souls decided to embark upon new careers with no idea of what awaited them.

These Brownists, who later were known as Pilgrims, were only one group of the many people who suffered persecution in Europe in the seventeenth century during the general wave of intolerance that brought about the democratic revolts. In England Catholics had been harassed by Thomas Cromwell, and Protestants by Mary Tudor. From 1629 to 1640 Puritan and Catholic families fled to America, and when the Stuarts were restored in 1660 the exodus was renewed, with such sects as the Quakers joining the emigration.

It is interesting to us, in our study of our *Mayflower* ancestors, to realize what a long way they had to go before they could come to the crystallization of the Democratic theory through the Declaration of Independence and the Bill of Rights.

The first *Mayflower* Contract, signed in the *Mayflower* before the Pilgrims landed in this country provided:

"We, whose names are underwritten, covenant and combine ourselves together into a civil body politic for our better ordering and preservation and furtherance of the ends aforesaid; and to enact, constitute and frame such just and equal laws, ordinances, etc., from time to time as shall be thought most fair and convenient for the general good of the colony to which we promise all due submission and obedience." The interest to me in this first document is the acceptance of self-discipline.

The Fundamental Orders of Connecticut provided that: "there shall be two yearly general assemblies, one in April and one in September. The first shall be called the Court of Election wherein so many magistrates and other public officers shall be chosen, one to be chosen governor for the ensuing year or until another governor shall be chosen, and always six others beside the governor who shall have the power to administer justice according to the laws here established, and for want thereof, according to the rule of the Word of God. This choice shall be made by all that are admitted freemen and have taken the oath of fidelity and live within this jurisdiction.

"Every person present and qualified for choice shall bring in to persons deputed to receive them, one single paper on which is written the name of the man he desires to have as governor, and he who has the greatest number of papers shall be governor for that year.

"For the others to be elected, the secretary shall read the names and nominate them and everyone shall bring in one single paper with a name written on it, and the one who receives the most written papers, is elected for that year.

"No person shall be chosen governor above one in two years, and the governor must be a member of some approved congregation.

"The general court in September shall be for making laws and any other public occasion, which concerns the good of the commonwealth.

"Each town is empowered to send four freemen as deputies and such deputies shall have power to give their votes to all such laws and orders as may be for the public good and these laws shall bound the towns.

"Such deputies shall have the power and liberty to appoint a time and place of meeting together to advise and consult on all such things as may concern the good of the public, to examine their own elections, and if they are found illegal they may be excluded from the meetings. These deputies to have the power to fine any one who was disorderly at the meetings, for not coming in due time.

"The General Court to consist of the governor, or someone chosen to moderate the court and four other magistrates at least with the major part of the deputies of the several towns legally chosen. If the governor and the major part of the magistrates refuse or neglect to call a court, it shall consist of the major part of freemen that are present or their deputies with a moderator chosen by them. Said General Court shall have power to make laws, or repeal them, grant levies, admit freemen, dispose of lands, and may deal in any other matter that concerns the good of the commonwealth except election of magistrates which shall be done by the whole body of freemen.

"In this court the governor or moderator shall have power to order the court, to give liberty of speech, and silence unreasonable and disorderly speakings, to put all things to vote and in the case of a tie vote, have the casting vote. The courts shall not be adjourned or dissolved without the consent of the major part of the court.

"The court may agree on sum or sums of money to be levied on the several towns within its jurisdiction, and a committee chosen to decide what shall be the proportion of every town of the levy, provided the committee be made up of an equal number from each town." Here we find mentioned for the first time "The rule of the Word of God."

The Fundamental Articles of Rhode Island stated that those who had signed their names, promised to subject themselves in obedience to all orders or agreements which were made for the public good, in an orderly way, by the major consent of the present inhabitants incorporated together into a town fellowship.

This compact in some ways resembles the *Mayflower* Compact, except that in the above, obedience is promised in civil things only, and the term civil is used in contradistinction to ecclesiastical. Obedience is promised in matters pertaining to the state and not to those pertaining to the church.

William Penn's Limited Democratic State was extreme republicanism. He abolished all rules of inheritance, gave all the power to the people to initiate and repeal laws, reserving no veto for himself. All taxes were to be collected by law, the courts were to be open and no oaths required. Penalties were light, capital punishment abolished except for murder (this was remarkable because there were two hundred offenses in the English law which carried the death sentence), prisons were to be workhouses and all children taught a useful trade. All those who professed faith in Jesus Christ were to be eligible to office, and all who confessed an Almighty God were to have free exercise of their worship. In some respects this document was changed, but the one feature to which Penn clung tenaciously was wide religious liberty. The faith in Jesus Christ as here expressed is, I think, the beginning of an idea that this faith would influence the life of the individual and make him better able to meet Penn's standards as a citizen.

Americans led the way in the development of Democracy, and through the first three-quarters of the eighteenth century, certain men developed the thought of the people of this country, and prepared for the Revolutionary War. The Revolutionary War in this country was the first real proof that the theory of Democracy could command the loyalty of a body of citizens and did not require an individual as a ruler to tie the government together.

These "radicals" who prepared for our Revolution were Thomas Paine, Patrick Henry, Samuel Adams and James Otis.

Thomas Paine is, of course, best known for his writings. His pamphlet "Common Sense," arguing for the separation of the American colonies, published in 1776, had powerful effect. This was the first time the republican doctrines in politics which were inseparable from the individualist trend of the Protestant Reformation in religion had been put down in popular form. He gave practical ideas of representative government, and almost at once the theory upon which our government was to be laid was in every man's mind.

Paine's "The Rights of Man," published in

parts, the first in 1791, stated the fundamental principles for representative republicanism, in language which everyone could understand, and so cheaply that everyone could read it. The tide of opinion was caught, and "The Rights of Man" made Paine the leader of the republicans in France and the radicals in England.

"The Age of Reason" by Paine contrasts the Bible as absolute truth with the Bible in the light of scientific knowledge and the common sense of the time. It was a break with organized religion, in the train of thought that led to Unitarianism, and to such movements as the Ethical Culture Society. Paine wrote to be read by the people and the people read him. In self-protection the English and American church institutions turned Paine into the Devil himself. This embittered Paine and deprived the Republicans in America of the full use of his great experience and of his talents as a political commentator. Hitler's campaign against the Jews is comparable to the campaign in England against free-thinkers and infidels.

Patrick Henry urged the colonists to go to war on March 20, 1775, at the second convention assembled in Richmond, Virginia, and up to that time no public body or public man had openly spoken of a war with Great Britain. They had admitted that it was highly probable, but not inevitable. He proposed resolutions which were passed.

Samuel Adams was one of the most important men in the work which was done to convince the colonists that they were oppressed. He came into prominence with the passing of the Sugar Act in 1764. From this time almost every state paper in Massachusetts and the initiation of almost every great measure can be traced to him.

James Otis gained public notice by pleading the cause of the Writs of Assistance. His oratory sowed the seeds of the Declaration of Independence and the American Revolution. He was an original political thinker and while he was an imperialist, it was upon natural law as conceived by Otis that the American Revolution was finally defended.

The results of this preparation of American thought flowered in such men as Thomas Jefferson, James Madison, George Mason and the others who helped to write the Declaration of Independence and then to argue for its acceptance as the basis of the establishment of a new type of government.

The Declaration of Independence and the Constitution were documents with completely different purposes. The Declaration of Independence embodies the beliefs in Democracy and the theories of the people of that day. The Constitution grew out of the practical minds of the men who fought the Revolution and who realized that they must consolidate the government of this small group of people, who had decided to be free, into something workable and unified.

The Constitution itself, argued out in the Constitutional Conventions of the day, shows the fears that many men had of Democracy. Many of its provisions tended to safeguard the state from too much power in the hands of the people. This brought about the demand for the Bill of Rights which contains the Amendments to guard the people's idea of Democracy, thus winning the adoption of the Constitution which created a nation.

Jefferson protested loudly against a system of government which gave governors the power to take from the citizens the right to a trial by jury, freedom of religion, freedom of the press, freedom of commerce, the habeas corpus laws. He insisted that the people were entitled to a Bill of Rights against every government on earth.

Patrick Henry said a Bill of Rights "is an indispensable necessity," and a greater necessity in the form of government which was set up in the United States than in any other, if the people wished to keep their inalienable rights.

Purposely the Constitution was left flexible to meet the future needs of the nation. It was recognized by the forward-looking men of that day that these needs would change, and in that they have been proven far-seeing statesmen, for the mere fact that we have been obliged to add amendments to the Constitution from time to time proves that flexibility was necessary.

Benjamin Franklin said about the Constitution:
"I confess that there are several parts of this Constitution which I do not at present approve, but I am not sure I shall never approve them; for, having lived long, I have experienced many instances of being obliged by better information or fuller consideration to change opinions, even on important subjects, which I once thought right but found to be otherwise.

"It is therefore that the older I grow the more apt I am to doubt my own judgment and to pay attention to the judgment of others. Most men, indeed, as well as most sects in religion think themselves in possession of all truth. . . . But though many private persons think almost as highly of their infallibility as of that of their sect, few express it so naturally as a certain French lady who in a dispute with her sister said: 'I don't know how it happens sister, but I meet with nobody but myself that's always in the right.'

"In these sentiments, Sir, I agree to this Constitution with all its faults, if they are such; because I think a general government necessary for us, and there is no form of government but what may be a blessing to the people if well administered; and believe further that this is likely to be well administered for a course of years and can only end in despotism, as other forms have done before it, when the people shall become so corrupt as to need despotic government, being incapable of any other.

"I doubt too, whether any other convention we can obtain may be able to make a better Constitution. For when you assemble a number of men to have the advantage of their joint wisdom, you inevitably assemble with those men all their prejudices, their passions, their errors of opinion, their local interests, and their selfish views. From such an assembly can a perfect production be expected? It therefore astonishes me, Sir, to find this system approaching so near to perfection as it does. . . .

"Thus I consent, Sir, to this Constitution because I expect no better, and because I am not sure that it is not the best. The opinions I have had of its errors I sacrifice to the public good. I have never whispered a syllable of them abroad. Within these walls they were born, and here they shall die. . . . On the whole, Sir, I can not help expressing a wish that every member of the Convention who may still have objections to it would, with me, on this occasion doubt a little of his infallibility, and, to make manifest our unanimity, put his name to this instrument."

We cannot reread the above often enough, for it holds priceless lessons for us all. Franklin understood human beings, and he knew the extent to which we must all compromise when we come together to formulate plans for the public good.

It was evident, however, that the rights of the individual had to be obtained by continuous vigilance in those days just as the rights can only be maintained today in the same way. So it is interesting to find it stated in James S. Allen's book that Paine, who left for Europe in 1787, before the Constitutional Convention convened and who is considered to be the author of the Declaration of the Rights of Man, issued by the French National Assembly in 1789, succeeded in having incorporated in that document many of the guiding principles of the American Declaration of Independence. Here was a bill of rights such as Jefferson and the American Democrats fought to have included in the American Constitution and which was finally added in the form of the first ten amendments.

Note this "Declaration of the Rights of Man and of Citizen by the National Assembly of France," as given in John Dos Passos' book on Tom Paine.

1. Men are born, and always continue, free and equal in respect to their rights. Civil distinctions, therefore, can be founded only on public utility.

2. The end of all political associations, is, the preservation of the natural and imprescriptible

rights of man; and these rights are liberty, property, security, and resistance of oppression.

3. The nation is essentially the source of all sovereignty; nor can any individual, or any body of men, be entitled to any authority which is not expressly derived from it.

4. Political liberty consists in the power of doing whatever does not injure another. The exercise of the natural rights of every man has no other limits than those which are necessary to secure to every other man the free exercise of the same rights; and these limits are determinable only by law.

5. The law ought to prohibit only actions hurtful to society. What is not prohibited by the law, should not be hindered; nor should any one be compelled to that which the law does not require.

6. The law is an expression of the will of the community. All citizens have a right to concur, either personally, or by their representatives, in its formation. It should be the same to all, whether it protects or punishes; and all being equal in its sight, are equally eligible to all honors, places and

employments, according to their different abilities, without any other distinction than that created by their virtues and talents.

7. No man should be accused, arrested, or held in confinement, except in cases determined by the law, and according to the forms which it has prescribed. All who promote, solicit, execute, or cause to be executed, arbitrary orders, ought to be punished; and every citizen called upon or apprehended by virtue of the law, ought immediately to obey, and renders himself culpable by resistance.

8. The law ought to impose no other penalties but such as are absolutely and evidently necessary; and no one ought to be punished but in virtue of a law promulgated before the offense, and legally applied.

9. Every man being presumed innocent till he has been convicted, whenever his detention becomes indispensable, all rigour to him, more than is necessary to secure his person, ought to be provided against by the law.

10. No man ought to be molested on account

of his opinions, not even on account of his religious opinions, provided his avowal of them does not disturb the public order established by the law.

11. The unrestrained communication of thoughts and opinions being one of the most precious rights of man, every citizen may speak, write, and publish freely, provided he is responsible for the abuse of this liberty in cases determined by the law.

12. A public force being necessary to give security to the rights of men and of citizens, that force is instituted for the benefit of the community, and not for the particular benefit of the persons with whom it is entrusted.

13. A common contribution being necessary for the support of the public force, and for defraying the other expenses of government, it ought to be divided equally among the members of the community, according to their abilities.

14. Every citizen has a right, either by himself or his representative, to a free voice in determining the necessity of public contributions, the ap-

propriation of them, and their amount, mode of assessment and duration.

15. Every community has a right to demand of all its agents, an account of their conduct.

16. Every community in which a separation of powers and a security of rights is not provided for, wants a constitution.

17. The rights of property being inviolable and sacred, no one ought to be deprived of it, except in cases of evident public necessity, legally ascertained, and on condition of a previous just indemnity.

An Englishman, Francis W. Hirst, in his "Life and Letters of Thomas Jefferson," quotes a passage which shows Jefferson's appreciation of the part Tom Paine played in preparing our people for Democracy. Jefferson wrote:

"The soil for the seed of independence . . . was sown broadcast by Tom Paine's 'Common Sense,' one of the most powerful and influential pamphlets ever published in the English language. It appeared on January 10, 1776 . . . 'Common Sense' ran like wildfire through the Colonies. It shattered the King's cause by setting forth in simple language the virtues of Democracy, the utility of independence, and the absurdity of submitting to the arbitrary rule of an hereditary tyrant. To the conservative and slow-moving mind of Washington its doctrine seemed 'sound' and its reasoning 'unanswerable'. Within three months 120,000 copies had passed into circulation, and the lingering doubts of many plain peaceable folk reluctant to break with Britain were dispelled."

France sent men over to participate in our Revolution primarily, of course, because of her antagonism to England, but among those who came were men, who, like Lafayette, were fighting for the theory of Democracy. The French Revolution which followed ours may have gained impetus because of our example. After the French Revolution in 1789, the calling of the Estates General in France is the first instance of universal manhood suffrage.

# 3.

UNDER OUR Constitution, the union established was really a republic with a representative form of government and a series of checks and balances to control the various arms of government as well as the people of the country.

While the Revolution was produced by the agitation of Paine, Otis, Adams, and others, the first individuals who came to power under our republican form of government were Washington,

Hamilton, John Adams, John Jay—all of them conservatives, well rooted in English traditions.

With the arrival in power of the radicals, the reform group headed by Jefferson, Madison, Duane, and others, we find a change in the theory of our republican form of government and the crystallization and stabilization of some of the beliefs of what political Democracy must eventually recognize.

Jefferson believed in the honesty and ability of the average man, regardless of his social position, education, wealth and other opportunities. Jefferson's position is explicitly stated in the second paragraph of the Declaration of Independence:

"We hold these truths to be self-evident, that all men are created equal; that they are endowed by their Creator with certain inalienable rights; that among these are life, liberty and the pursuit of happiness." Jefferson believed in the education of all classes, and a government with a minimum of power that would not infringe too much on the independence and liberty of a free and active individual. He was for the freeing of the slaves.

In Jefferson's beliefs we get the clearest statements for his day of a true understanding of human beings. He wanted no slaves because he realized that slavery was the denial of the equality of man. It meant that if we denied equality to any man we lost the basis of Democracy. If we are honest with ourselves today, we will acknowledge that the ideal of Democracy has never failed, but that we haven't carried it out, and in our lack of faith we have debased the human being who must have a chance to live if Democracy is to be successful.

The slave is still with us, but his color is not always black, and I think we will also have to acknowledge that most of our difficulties arise today from the fact that in the rush of material development we have neglected to keep close enough to the Revolutionary idea, guided by religious feeling, which is the basis of Democracy. We have undertaken, under our form of government, to carry out the ideal which can exist only if we accept the brotherhood of man as a basic truth in human society.

We may belong to any religion or to none, but we must acknowledge that the life of Christ was based on principles which are necessary to the development of a Democratic state. We accept that fact and measure every undertaking by that rule. But, it is easy to understand where our difficulties lie today. Even Thomas Paine said: "The rights of property being inviolate and sacred, no one ought to be deprived of it, except in cases of evident public necessity, legally ascertained, and on condition of a previous indemnity."

*Our present situation, our present difficulties arise from the fact that in the development of civilization we have neglected to remember that the rights of all people to some property are inviolate. We have allowed a situation to arise where many people are debased by poverty or the accident of race, in our own country, and therefore have no stake in Democracy; while others appeal to this old rule of the sacredness of prop-*

erty rights to retain in the hands of a limited number the fruits of the labor of many.

We have never been willing to face this problem, to line it up with the basic, underlying beliefs in Democracy and to set our actions side by side with the actual example of the Christ-like way of living.

Thus, within our nation there are many who do not understand the values of Democracy, and we have been unable to spread these values throughout the world, because as a people we have been led by the gods of Mammon from the spiritual concepts and from the practical carrying-out of those concepts conceived for our nation as a truly free and democratic people.

## 4.

WHAT ARE OUR problems today?

I have reviewed the past and pointed out the association of a Christ-like life to the Democratic ideal of government, inaugurated to produce a Democratic way of life.

Now, let us look at our country as it is today and see if, from this examination, we can get a better understanding of some of our problems, and some of the decisions which we have got to make in the near future.

First of all we are a great nation of 130,000,000 people. We cover about three million, seven hundred thousand square miles, including our outlying dependencies such as the Philippines, Puerto Rico, the Virgin Islands, etc. Our people stem from every nation in the world. We include Orientals, Negroes, Europeans, Latin-Americans. We are in truth the melting pot of the world. Our solidarity and unity can never be a geographical unity or a racial unity. It must be a unity growing out of a common idea and a devotion to that idea.

Our national income last year, 1939, was $69,378,000,000. It went down as low as $40,074,000,000 in 1932 in contrast with the peak in 1929, which was $82,885,000,000.

We are slowly climbing out of the economic morass we fell into, but so long as we have the number of unemployed on our hands which we have today, we can be sure that our ecomonic troubles are not over and that we have not found the permanent solution to our problem.

There is going to be almost an entire continent of vast natural resources under the direction of an

45

opposing philosophy to ours, and an opposing economic system. Either we must make our economic system work to the satisfaction of all of our people, or we are going to find it extremely difficult to compete against the one which will be set up on the Continent of Europe.

We hear a good deal of loose talk about going to war. As a matter of fact we are already in a war—an economic war and a war of philosophies. We are opposing a force which, under the rule of one man, completely organizes all business and all individuals and takes no chances except with such uncontrollable phenomena as weather, fire, flood or earthquake. This one man in Europe has no limit on what he can spend for the things he desires to bring about. If he wants quantities of armament, he simply goes ahead and has quantities of armament. His nation has functioned on an internal currency. When he has need for things from outside, he has obtained them by barter of his manufactured goods or by simply taking the gold which he needed to buy goods from other nations, from those who happened to have it in his own country or from some other country that he decided to take over.

His people receive the wages *he* decrees, they work the hours *he* decrees, they wear the clothes *he* allows them to wear, they eat the food *he* allows them to have. They go away or do not go away for vacations according to his caprice, and they take no vacations outside of their own country without his permission, and even when a visit outside their own country is permitted, they can take only a specified sum of money with them.

An effort to set up similar conditions is quite evidently being made by Japan in the Far East. Our entire continent must be aroused to what it will mean if these ideas are successful. Our Democracies must realize that from the point of view of the individual and his liberty, there is no hope in the future if the totalitarian philosophy becomes dominant in the world.

Here, in this country, it seems to me that as the strongest nation in the battle today, we have to take an account of just what our condition is; how much Democracy we have and how much we want to have.

It is often said that we are free, and then sneeringly it is added: "free to starve if we wish." In some parts of our country that is no idle jest. Moreover, no one can honestly claim that either the Indians or the Negroes of this country are free. These are obvious examples of conditions which are not compatible with the theory of Democracy. We have poverty which enslaves, and racial prejudice which does the same. There are other racial and religious groups among us who labor under certain discriminations, not quite so difficult as those we impose on the Negroes and the Indians, but still sufficient to show we do not completely practice the Democratic way of life.

It is quite obvious that we do not practice a Christ-like way of living in our relationship to submerged people, and here again we see that a kind of religion which gives us a sense of obligation about living with a deeper interest in the welfare of our neighbors is an essential to the success of Democracy.

# 5.

WE ARE, of course, going through a type of revolution and we are succeeding in bringing about a greater sense of social responsibility in the people as a whole. Through the recognition by our government of a responsibility for social conditions much has been accomplished; but there is still much to be done before we are even prepared to accept some of the fundamental facts which will make it possible to fight as a unified nation against the new philosophies arrayed in opposition to Democracy.

It would seem clear that in a Democracy a minimum standard of security must at least be possible for every child in order to achieve the equality of opportunity which is one of the basic principles set forth as a fundamental of Democracy. This means achieving an economic level below which no one is permitted to fall, and keeping a fairly stable balance between that level and the cost of living. No one as yet seems to know just how to do this without an amount of planning which will be considered too restrictive for freedom. The line between domination and voluntary acquiescence in certain controls is a very difficult one to establish. Yet it is essential in a Democracy.

For a number of years we seemed to be progressing toward a condition in which war as a method of settling international difficulties might be eliminated, but with the rise of an opposing philosophy of force, this has become one of our main problems today. It brings before us the question of whether under the Democratic theory we can be efficient enough to meet the growing force of totalitarianism with its efficient organization for aggression.

This question is of special interest to youth, and added to the question of unemployment, it creates for them the main problem of existence.

The youth which is coming of age in our country today is living under a government which is attempting to meet a great many internal problems in new ways, and with methods never before tried. These ways are questioned by a great many people; but few people question the fact that the problems are with us and must be faced.

Youth seems to be more conscious than anyone else of the restrictions of opportunity which have come with our form of civilization. Some of these restrictions may be due to the development of the nation to a degree which leaves few physical frontiers to master; some of them may be due to a lack of social development, to a system which hasn't kept pace with the machine and made it possible to use advantageously more leisure time.

Such mal-functioning makes it impossible to lessen the burden of labor without curtailing the volume of work, so that many people are left with nothing to do, and therefore without the wherewithal for living.

Nowhere in the world today has government solved these questions. Therefore, as their elders leave the stage, it remains for youth to find a way to face the domestic situation, to meet the conditions which confront their country in its relationship with the other countries of the world.

It is not enough to adopt the philosophies and methods which have appeared in other countries. These difficulties have been met elsewhere by deciding that one man who orders the lives of great numbers of people can best arrange for the equable distribution of the necessities of life. From the point of view of our Democratic philosophy and our belief in the welfare of the individual this has fatal drawbacks.

Youth must make a decision. It will have to decide whether religion, the spirit of social cooperation, is necessary to the development of a

Democratic form of government and to the relationship which human beings must develop if they are to live happily together. If it is, Youth will have to devise some means of bringing it more closely to the hearts and to the daily lives of everyone.

It is not entirely the fault of any of the churches, or of any of the various religious denominations that so many people, who call themselves Catholic, Protestant or Jew, behave as though religion were something shut up in one compartment of their lives. It seems to have no effect on their actions or their growth or on their relationship to their surroundings and activities.

Leaders of religious thought have tried for generations to make us understand that religion is a way of life which develops the spirit. Perhaps, because of the circumstances which face us today, the youth of this generation may make this type of religion a reality. I think they might thus develop for the future of this country and of the world a conception of success which will change our whole attitude toward life and civilization.

# 6.

YOUTH WISHES to do away with war. But youth and the men and women of Democracy will have to set their own house in order first, and show that they have something to offer under a Democratic form of government which is not offered by any other philosophy or any other theory of government.

It will be an exciting new world if it is created on these principles. It will not mean that great changes take place overnight, because people have been born for generations under conditions which it will take generations to change; but a new concept held by the youth of today as a basic meaning of Democracy, and its foundations in a religion, which shows itself in actual ways of life, will, I think, change the future generations.

We cannot expect, of course, that any development will go on without some setbacks, and we are at present in one of the most serious of retrogressions. If any of the young people of 1917 and 1918 could return to us today they would undoubtedly feel that the sacrifice of their lives had been valueless. Yet, I have a feeling that perhaps in the long run that sacrifice will be the one thing that will drive the young generation of today into doing something which will permanently change the future. They know that a gesture of self-sacrifice is not enough; that they cannot in one war change the basic things which have produced wars. They know that they must begin with human beings and keep on, each in his or her own particular sphere of influence, building up a social conscience and a sense of responsibility for their neighbors. They have begun to build bridges between the youth of their own nation and the youth of other nations. These bridges may be stronger because of the fiery trials so many young people are going through today. The value of human liberty may have a more tangible meaning to the next generation than it has in the present because for so many human beings it has temporarily disappeared.

The challenge of today is, I think, the greatest challenge that youth has faced in many generations. The future of Democracy in this country lies with them, and the future of Democracy in the world lies with them as well. The development of a dynamic Democracy which is alive and actively working for the benefit of all individuals, and not for just a few, depends, I think, on the realization that this form of government is not a method devised to keep some particular group that is stronger than other groups in power. It is a method of government conceived for the development of human beings as a whole.

The citizens of a Democracy must model themselves on the best and most unselfish life we have known in history. They may not all believe in Christ's divinity, though many will; but His life is important simply because it becomes a shining beacon of what success means. If we once establish this human standard as a measure of success, the future of Democracy is secure.

# 7.

THE WAR-RIDDEN, poverty-stricken world of today seems to be struggling essentially with problems of economics and its ills seem to be primarily materialistic. Yet, I believe that we do not begin to approach a solution of our problems until we acknowledge the fact that they are spiritual and that they necessitate a change in the attitude of human beings to one another.

War is the result of spiritual poverty. People say that war is the cause of a great many of our troubles; but in the first analysis it is the fact that human beings have not developed the ability to rise above purely selfish interest which brings about war. Then war intensifies all of our social problems and leaves us groping for the answers.

As we look at France today we realize that her plight is partly due to the fact that some of her people actually believed that the Communists were more of a menace than the Fascists. Both were an equal menace, for their hold on the people comes from the same sources—discontent and insecurity. The people who were comfortably off never looked below the surface in France to find out why the Communists could get such a hold on the imagination of people in a country which had supposedly so much liberty and equality.

Some people say salvation can come only through a form of selfish interest which brings about the realization by those who have their share of the good things of life, that nothing which they have in a material sense will be preserved unless they share it with those less fortunate; that some charitable way will be found to distribute more equably the things which the people as a whole lack. This would be a reaction to fear, of course, and it does not seem to me a final answer.

Somehow or other, human beings must get a feeling that there is in life a spring, a spring which flows for all humanity, perhaps like the old legendary spring from which men drew eternal youth. This spring must fortify the soul and give people a vital reason for wanting to meet the problems of the world today, and to meet them in a way which will make life more worth living for everyone. It must be a source of social inspiration and faith.

It is quite true, perhaps, that "Whom the Lord loveth, He chasteneth"; but nowhere is it said that individual human beings shall chasten each other, and it seems to me that all of us are sufficiently chastened by the things which are beyond our power to change. We can do nothing about death, or physical disabilities which science does not understand and cannot therefore remedy; nor can we help the maladjustments of various kinds which lie in the personality and not in the physical surroundings of the individual.

So the chastening will come to us all, rich and poor alike. But hunger and thirst, lack of decent shelter, lack of certain minimum decencies of life, can be eliminated if the spirit of good will is awakened in every human being.

# 8.

I AM NOT writing a political thesis, otherwise I might explain how we have been groping for a way during the past few years, to achieve some of these ends through government. In this little book, however, I am trying to go a little bit deeper and point out that court decisions, and laws and government administration are only the results of the way people progress inwardly, and that the basis of success in a Democracy is really laid down by the people. It will progress only as their own personal development goes forward.

When I have occasionally said to people that perhaps some of us had too much of this world's goods, and that we are thereby separated too widely from each other and unable to understand the daily problems of people in more limited circumstances, I have often been met by the argument that these more privileged people are the ones who open up possibilities and new vistas for others. They are the people, I am told, who because of greater leisure have developed an appreciation of art; they build art galleries and museums, and give to other people an opportunity to enjoy them. They are the people who could envision the possibilities of scientific research, thereby building up great research laboratories where students make discoveries which increase our knowledge along so many lines. They are the people who create foundations which help the unfortunates of the world. All this is true, and we must be grateful for it, but perhaps it is time to take a new step in the progress of humanity.

I wonder if part of our education does not still lie before us and if we should not think of educating every individual to the need of making a contribution for these purposes which have been recognized only by a small group in the past as their contribution to society. The development of art, science, and literature for the benefit of our country as a whole is a concern of the whole country, not of a privileged few. I wonder if the support for these things should not come through an infinite number of small gifts rather than through a few great ones.

I recognize the fact that this development is slow and in some ways may be a question of years of evolution, particularly until we approach the better understanding of people of different races and different creeds. This country is perhaps the best example, however, of the fact that all people can learn to live side by side. We have here representatives of almost every nation and almost every religious belief.

There have been times when waves of bigotry

and intolerance have swept over us. There is still a lack of true appreciation of the contributions made by some of these nations to the development of our culture, but the fact remains that, by and large, we live happily and understandingly together and gradually amalgamate until it is hard to distinguish what was once a separate nationality and what is today entirely a product of the United States of America.

This should give us courage to realize that there can be a real development of understanding among human beings, though it may take a great many years before there is sufficient change throughout the world to eliminate some of the dangers which we now face daily. There must be a beginning to all things and it seems to me the beginning for a better world understanding might well be made right here. Our natural resources are very great, and are still far from being fully developed. Our population is mixed and we are still young enough to be responsive to new ideas and to make changes fairly easily.

Some people feel that human nature cannot

be changed, but I think when we look at what has been achieved by the Nazi and Fascist dictators we have to acknowledge the fact that we do not live in a static condition, but that the influences of education, of moral and physical training have an effect upon our whole beings. If human beings can be changed to fit a Nazi or Fascist pattern or a Communist pattern, certainly we should not lose heart at the thought of changing human nature to fit a Democratic way of life.

# 9.

PEOPLE SAY that the churches have lost their hold and that therein is found one of our greatest difficulties. Perhaps they have, but if that is true, it is because the churches have thought about the churches and not about religion as a need for men to live by. Each man may have his own religion; the church is merely the outward and visible symbol of the longing of the human soul for something to which he can aspire and which he desires beyond his own strength to achieve.

If human beings can be trained for cruelty and greed and a belief in power which comes through hate and fear and force, certainly we can train equally well for gentleness and mercy and the power of love which comes because of the strength of the good qualities to be found in the soul of every individual human being.

While force is abroad in the world we may have to use that weapon of force, but if we develop the fundamental beliefs and desires which make us considerate of the weak and truly anxious to see a Christ-like spirit on earth, we will have educated ourselves for Democracy in much the same way that others have gone about educating people for other purposes. We will have established something permanent because it has as its foundation a desire to sacrifice for the good of others, a trait which has survived in some human beings in one form or another since the world began.

We live under a Democracy, under a form of government which above all other forms should make us conscious of the need we all have for this spiritual, moral awakening. It is not something which must necessarily come through any one religious belief, or through people who go regularly to church and proclaim themselves as members of this or that denomination. We may belong to any denomination, we may be strict observers of certain church customs or we may be neglectful of forms, but the fundamental thing which we must all have is the spiritual force which the life of Christ exemplifies. We might well find it in the life of Buddha, but as long as it translates itself into something tangible in aspirations for ourselves and love for our neighbors, we should be content; for then we know that human nature is struggling toward an ideal.

Real Democracy cannot be stable and it cannot go forward to its fullest development and growth if this type of individual responsibility does not exist, not only in the leaders but in the people as a whole.

It is vitally important in the leaders because they are articulate. They should translate their aspirations and the means by which they wish to reach them, into clear words for other people to understand. In the past I think they have never dared to voice all their dreams, they have never dared to tell all the people their hopes because of the fear that the people would not be able to see the same vision. Unless there is understanding behind a leader, and a compelling desire on the part of the people to go on, he must fail.

This Democratic experiment of ours is in its infancy; in fact, real Democracy has never been realized, because it involves too much individual responsibility, and we have been slow to accept it.

Democracy does not imply, of course, that each and every individual shall achieve the same status in life, either materially or spiritually; that is not reasonable because we are limited by the gifts with which we enter this world. It does mean, however, that each individual should have the chance, because of the standards we have set, for good health, equal education and equal opportunity to achieve success according to his powers; and this opportunity should exist in whatever line of work, either of hand or head, he may choose to engage in. It also means that through self-government each individual should carry his full responsibility; otherwise the Democracy can not be well balanced and represent the whole people.

I think that our estimate of success is going to change somewhat and that the man or woman who achieves a place in the community through service to the community will be considered a more successful individual than anyone who gains wealth or power which benefits himself alone. Changing the standards of success is going to mean more to the future of youth than anything else we can do, so perhaps this is the time for us to consider what is the future of youth.

# 10.

THERE ARE two questions which young people in our country have to face. What are we prepared to sacrifice in order to retain the Democratic form of government?

What do we gain if we retain this form of government?

Let us consider first the sacrifices that we make in a real Democracy. Our basic sacrifice is the privilege of thinking and working for ourselves alone. From time immemorial the attitude of the individual has been one of selfishness. As civilization has advanced people have thought of their families, and finally of a group of people like themselves; but down in our hearts it has always been the interest which you and I had in ourselves primarily which has motivated us.

If we are able to have genuine Democracy we are going to think primarily of the rights and privileges and the good that may come to the people of a great nation. This does not mean, of course, that we are going to find everyone in agreement with us in what we think is for the good of the majority of the people; but it does mean that we will be willing to submit our ideas to the test of what the majority wishes.

That is a big sacrifice for Democracy. It means that we no longer hold the fruits of our labors as our own, but consider them in the light of a trusteeship. Just as the labor itself must be put into avenues which may no longer be bringing us what at one time we considered as satisfactory returns, but which are serving some socially useful purpose in the community in which we live.

This does not mean that we will work any less hard. It does not mean that we will use less initiative or put less preparation into the field of work in which we are entering. It does mean, however, that we will execute to the best of our ability every piece of work which we undertake and give our efforts to such things as seem to us to serve the purposes of the greatest number of people.

The second sacrifice which we make for Democracy is to give to our government an interested and intelligent participation. For instance, if a city, town or county meeting is called, we will not find something more interesting or attractive to do that evening. We will go to the meeting, take part in it and try to understand what the questions and issues are. Thus we start the machinery of Democracy working from the lowest rung upward.

We often make the mistake of believing that what happens at the bottom makes no difference. As a matter of fact, it is what we do at the bottom which decides what eventually happens at the top. If all the way down the line every able-bodied citizen attended to his duties, went to the community meetings, tried to find out about the people who were going to hold office, knew the questions that came before them, there would be a radical change in the quality of people who take active part in political work.

We must have party machinery because there must be people who attend to such things as calling meetings, sending out notices, going from door to door to distribute literature or bring the issues to the voters before Election Day. These issues can be presented in many different ways, according to the understanding and the feeling of the people who present them. It would not be so difficult to find people to run for office if we knew that the citizens as a whole were going to know something about them and their ideas, and were going to vote not on a traditional basis, but according to their actual knowledge of the questions at stake and the personalities of the candidates. There would be less opportunity for calumny, for unfairness, and for the acceptance of untrue statements if, every step of the way, each individual took his responsibility seriously and actually did his job as a citizen in a Democracy.

There is no reward for this kind of citizenship except the reward of feeling that we really have a government which in every way represents the best thought of all the citizens involved. In such a Democracy a man will hold office not because it brings certain honors and considerations from his constituents, but because he has an obligation to perform a service to Democracy.

Perhaps the greatest sacrifice of all is the necessity which Democracy imposes on every individual to make himself decide in what he believes. If we believe in Democracy and that it is based on the possibility of a Christ-like way of life, then everybody must force himself to think through his own basic philosophy, his own willingness to live up to it and to help carry it out in everyday living.

The great majority of people accept religious dogmas handed to them by their parents without very much feeling of having a personal obligation to clarify their creed for themselves. But, if from our religion, whatever it may be, we are impelled to work out a way of life which leads to the support of a Democratic form of government, then we have a problem we cannot escape: we must know what we believe in, how we intend to live, and what we are doing for our neighbors.

Our neighbors, of course, do not include only the people whom we know; they include, also, all those who live anywhere within the range of our knowledge. That means an obligation to the coal miners and share-croppers, the migratory workers, to the tenement-house dwellers and the farmers who cannot make a living. It opens endless vistas of work to acquire knowledge and, when we have acquired it in our own country, there is still the rest of the world to study before we know what our course of action should be.

Again a sacrifice in time and thought, but a factor in a truly Democratic way of life.

Few members of the older generations have

even attempted to make of themselves the kind of people who are really worthy of the power which is vested in the individual in a Democracy. We must fulfill our duties as citizens, see that our nation is truly represented by its government, see that the government is responsive to the will and desires of the people. We must make that will and desire of the people the result of adequate education and adequate material security. We must maintain a standard of living which makes it possible for the people really to want justice for all, rather than to harbor a secret hope for privileges because they cannot hope for justice.

If we accomplish this, we have paved the way for the first hope for real peace the world has ever known. All people desire peace, but they are led to war because what is offered them in this world seems to be unjust, and they are constantly seeking a way to right that injustice.

These are the sacrifices future generations will be called upon to make for a permanent Democracy which has a background of spiritual belief.

# 11.

AND NOW, what do we gain from Democracy?

The greatest gain, perhaps, is a sense of brotherhood, a sense that we strive together toward a common objective.

I have sat with groups of people who for a few short minutes were united by the ideas and aspirations that had been presented to them by leaders able to express their vision or their dreams.

Those few minutes have made clear to me the

possibility of strength that some day might lie in a moral feeling of unity brought about by a true sense of brotherhood.

By achieving improvement in our own small sphere, we would gain, too, a tremendous satisfaction in realizing that we were actively participating in whatever happens in the world as a whole. The decisions at the top would be ours, because, in the first place, we had started choosing our men at the bottom and had thus brought about a real representation at the top. The new world which we conceived could become a reality, for these men, the leaders, would share the vision of the people.

It would be no Utopia, for the gains made by Democracy, which are the gains made by human beings over themselves, are never static. We fight for them and have to keep on fighting. The gains are slow and won in day by day effort. There is no chance for boredom or indifference because of a lack of further heights to climb. In such a society the heights are always before one, and the dread of slipping backward ever present.

One of the gains of Democracy would be that constant sense of vigilance and alertness which makes of life an adventure and gives it a continuous appeal. We cannot remove sorrow and disappointment from the lives of human beings, but we can give them an opportunity to free themselves from mass restrictions made by man.

There is nothing more exciting in the world than to be conscious of inwardly achieving something new; and anyone who puts into practice the life of Christ on earth, cannot fail to feel the growth in his own mastery over self. Under the Democracy based on such a religious impulse, there would still, of course, be leaders, and there would still be people of initiative interested and prodding other people to attempt the development of new ideas, or to participate in new enjoyments which they had not before understood or experienced.

Under such a Democracy the living standard of all the people would be gradually rising. That is what the youth of the next generation will be primarily interested in achieving, because that is the vital gain in Democracy for the future, if we base it on the Christian way of life as lived by the Christ.

DARTMOUTH COLLEGE

3 3311 00817 8271